Philosophy
of
Education
Workbook
Writing a Statement of
Beliefs and Practices

Jill Stamm
Caroline Wactler
Arizona State University

The McGraw-Hill Companies, Inc.
Primis Custom Publishing

800-338-3987

New York St. Louis San Francisco Auckland Bogotá
Caracas Lisbon London Madrid Mexico Milan Montreal
New Delhi Paris San Juan Singapore Sydney Tokyo Toronto

McGraw·Hill

A Division of The McGraw·Hill Companies

Philosophy of Education Workbook
Writing a Statement of Beliefs and Practices

McGraw-Hill's Primis Custom Series consists of products that are produced from camera-ready copy. Peer review, class testing, and accuracy are primarily the responsibility of the author(s).

1 2 3 4 5 6 7 8 9 0 GDP GDP 9 0 9 8 7

ISBN 0-07-109357-5

Editor: Lorna Adams
Cover Design: Maggie Lytle
Printer/Binder: Greyden Press

Table of Contents

◆ **Overview**   1
    Introduction   3
    The Purpose   4
    Philosophical Orientations   6
    Basic Tenets of Each Orientation   14

◆ **Exercises**   15
    Instructional Orientation Profile   16
    Example Philosophy Statements   17
    Philosophy Reflected in Educational Practices and Classroom Activities   20
    Philosophy Reflected in Policy Making   23
       Grading Policies   23
       Discipline Policies   26

◆ **Creating Your Philosophy of Education Statement**   29
    How to Write Your Statement   30
    Using Your Philosophy Statement in a Job Interview   37
    Conclusion   40

◆ **Appendix**   41
    Historical Roots of the Executive Approach   41
    Historical Roots of the Humanist Approach   42
    Historical Roots of the Classicist Approach   43
    Historical Roots of the Informationist Approach   44

◆ **Answer Key**   45

◆ **References**   48

On Philosophy...

"A successful leader has a basic philosophy. Your philosophy is simply an abstract statement of what you believe. Out of that belief you develop your methodology and your goals. But everything goes back to the philosophy."

–Tom Landry

Overview

◆ Introduction   3

◆ The Purpose   4

◆ Philosophical Orientations   6
    Executive   6
    Humanist   8
    Classicist   10
    Informationist   12

◆ Basic Tenets of Each Orientation   14

Introduction

Each of you will soon be starting the process of applying for your first teaching job. As you conclude your student teaching experience, you will need to **prepare a written statement of your philosophy of education** in order to complete applications for employment.

Preparing this philosophy statement and creating a resume, which is also typically required by employers, seem to be the most difficult tasks in the application process. There are numerous helpful resources for guidance in creating a resume. Books and self-help guides that provide tips and effective sample resumes are readily available for every conceivable employment category or job purpose. In addition, most universities offer special seminars on "How to Write a Resume" or they may maintain help desks within the Career Services office for resume preparation (Enz, 1997). If you take advantage of any of these offers, you will be left with only *one* unfinished task... writing your statement of educational philosophy.

Student teachers have reported varying degrees of stress resulting from this one remaining requirement ranging from mild anxiety, associated with the need to gather their thoughts on what they believe, to a virtual *halt* in completing the application. In order to finish the application it is not uncommon for students to resort to "filling" this blank paragraph (or on some district applications an entire page) with multisyllabic words that sound like someone's philosophy... but not necessarily theirs! This short term solution can have disastrous consequences because it is this statement that principals frequently use as a basis for formulating subsequent interview questions.

In this workbook, through brief explanations of various approaches to teaching and through written practice exercises and dialogue, you will be asked to identify and articulate your beliefs and attitudes about teaching and learning. This preliminary work will help you to write your educational philosophy statement.

The Purpose

The purpose of this workbook is to provide beginning instruction in philosophies of education. You will be introduced to just one of *several ways* that different approaches or philosophies of education can be categorized. You may wonder why you should know about several approaches when all you need in order to fill out the job application is *your* philosophical approach!

There are several reasons. First, learning how others approach teaching can help you to recognize where your style and beliefs fit into the larger picture. Many school districts across the country are in the process of divesting themselves of some of the district power and are creating site-based management school units that have greater decision making authority. This shift in power gives each building staff member exciting opportunities to influence the education of the students in that community. Critical choices about the focus of the individual school, the style of discipline, the grading system to be used, and the way the curriculum will be articulated are being made at the building level. It also brings basic questions such as: *What is an educated person? What is the role of the teacher? What are the goals of this school?* directly into the faculty lounge! Understanding "where someone else is coming from" may diffuse many heated, accusatory arguments. Only after knowing someone else's approach can you judge the effectiveness of what they do. Knowing one's purpose is essential to evaluating an outcome.

Second, you may have discovered during your student teaching that some of your on-the-job teaching behaviors differ from what you thought you believed philosophically or from what you were taught at the university. Or, depending on the circumstances, you may behave first one way and then another. It is perfectly normal, however, for beginning teachers to explore styles. As a new teacher your style is still evolving. New experiences will continue to inform you, and some of your beliefs will be modified. But you *do have* an existing belief structure. Your decision to become a teacher implies that you have a concept of what a teacher should be... of what you want to be.

There are some important general ways of thinking about your role as a teacher. Your particular conceptualization will have a tremendous effect on how you function on a day by day basis as a teacher, regardless of what subject or grade level you teach. Here are some things to consider:

◆ What you think good teaching *is* will effect your style (your tone or manner).
◆ What you think students should *become* as a result of your instruction will focus your efforts to help them achieve that aim.
◆ How you structure the learning atmosphere (environment) will reflect what you believe about teachers and students.

STOP...

Now, take a moment to complete the **Instructional Orientation Profile** (see pg. 16). Follow the instructions at the top of the page. After you have totaled the points in each column, you will notice that the total of one or two columns will be higher than the others. These scores will give you an indication of what your underlying beliefs and/or expectations are about education... at this time.

In this workbook, you will be learning four basic approaches to teaching. They are: the executive, the humanist, the classicist, and the informationist. The profile corresponds to these four approaches (Column 1 = Executive, 2 = Humanist, 3 = Classicist, 4 = Informationist). Perhaps few teachers would consider themselves purists in any one approach. You may determine that some aspects of your teaching behavior fit nicely into one approach but that other aspects of your behavior do not. That is normal. However, you will discover that in a broad sense, one of the four categories will "fit" you better than others. Each approach has several basic tenets that distinguish it from the others (see pg. 14). Take a look at the four approaches that are described on pages 6-13.

Philosophical Orientations

This traditional approach is labeled executive because it encompasses the efficiency many Americans are familiar with, and therefore, expect, when they think about classroom teaching. This approach is organized around the image of one teacher and 25-30 students in a classroom, and rests on the assumption that the teacher will impart her knowledge directly to the recipient students. The term executive, developed by David Berliner (1983), is thoroughly described in the text *Approaches to Teaching* (Fenstermacher & Soltis, 1992). The executive model is so labeled because it reflects many of the same values and outcomes that are found in business and industry.

As an executive, *the teacher is a manager* who is responsible for directing people, maximizing their efficiency, and focusing on end products that can be measured accurately. Common concerns tend to be quantitative and revolve around such questions as: "How many?" "How much?" "When?" The components of Madeline Hunter's Essential Elements of Instruction (Hunter 1971) are well understood by the executive teacher and are included in daily lesson planning.

District guidelines and grade level scope and sequence determine what will be taught. Similar to the curriculum development models of Tyler or Saylor, Alexander and Lewis (reported in Oliva, 1992), the executive teacher is very skill oriented, efficient in; lesson planning, devising materials to meet student needs, using motivational devices, testing to the objective and reteaching non-achieving students. The executive teacher reads and implements current research. The reason that teaching skills are important in the philosophical approach of this executive manager is that these techniques are used in the management of the classroom and in the production of learning.

In this paradigm, *the student is seen as the consumer of information.* The content to be learned is highly specified and is taught to students in the exact form they will need. The amount the student learns is always the chief concern. High achievement is the goal. The teacher controls the conditions for learning to insure that "information is moved from the source (text, lecture, etc.) directly to the destination (the student's mind)" (Fenstermacher, 1986, p. 15). This approach is decribed by Freire (1970, p. 64) as a "mechanistic" transfer of knowledge. There is a direct connection between what the teacher does and what the students learn.

The physical environment is structured in accordance with what contributes best to successful learning for a particular task. Group size, teaching methods and seating arrangement all vary depending on the teacher's decision of what is most efficient.

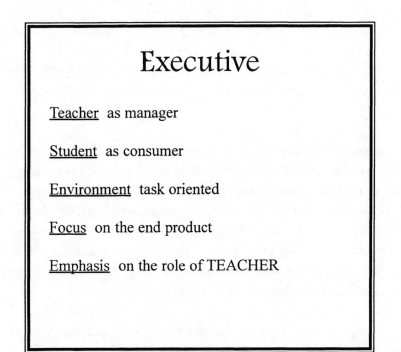

Executive

Teacher as manager

Student as consumer

Environment task oriented

Focus on the end product

Emphasis on the role of TEACHER

◆ *If you would like to read about the historical roots of these approaches, see Appendix.*

The humanist approach rests on the belief that learners' individual characteristics and histories influence their cognition. This approach shifts from the notion that information can be transferred, to a belief that information is selected by the learner in accordance with his/her motivation, prior knowledge and current needs.

The Humanist Approach

The humanist teacher is described by Fenstermacher and Soltis (1992) as reflecting a therapist philosophy. This approach to teaching emphasizes that the outcome of education should be a self-actualized person (Rogers, 1969, 1980; Maslow, 1970). This approach has its roots in the existential philosophy of Pestalozzi, Froebel, and Rousseau (Smith, 1984), and has as its focus the individual as the maker of meaning (Wactler, 1990).

The *role of the teacher* as humanist is as an empathetic person who *guides* the student in the process of discovering self. The teacher's task is clear. Teachers must prepare students to make good choices that will allow growth academically, socially and personally (Fenstermacher, 1986, p. 26).

The goal for a student as a self-actualized individual is to have a balanced and well-integrated personality. The teachers task is to direct the learner inward to seek personal meaning and identity. Because they are given continuous guidance and practice in making choices (Rogers, 1980), the students realize that they have choices about who and what they are. *Students, viewed as being at the center of the learning process,* are guided in how to make choices. They become active participants in choosing to acquire knowledge and skills that can help them to interpret their world.

To help in this process, the environment is organized to assure that information and relevant equipment is accessible to students. *The classroom environment is rich* with books, tapes, objects, animals, equipment, etc. The atmosphere is lively and independent. The learner chooses the content to be learned because, according to this approach, anything worthwhile is learned by oneself and not taught by someone else. The students' choice of what to learn and how to learn it is central to the humanist approach.

The humanist teacher is forthright and engaging with students. Teachers are honest about their own mistakes and weaknesses (Fenstermacher & Soltis, 1992). Learners are shown how to evaluate themselves. Equal opportunity for development is evident throughout the curriculum. By providing freedom, choice, and equality, the humanist approach seeks to create an independent and inventive society (Taba, 1962). What a person is and what they choose to become are most valued by the humanist teacher.

Humanist

Teacher as facilitator

Student as self-directed learner

Environment rich with multiple resources for students

Focus on self-actualization and exploration

Emphasis on the role of LEARNER

The Classicist Approach

The classicist approach has the greatest historical precedent, with its roots going back to ancient Greece. The emphasis of this approach is on content, at a high level of sophistication. Fenstermacher & Soltis (1992) refer to this approach as liberationist. As Paulo Freire (1970) writes, education can be the means to free the mind from the limits of everyday experience. In order to liberate the mind, exposure to specific classical works and philosophies is deemed crucial. There is emphasis on both depth and breadth of content. To be educated is to be well rounded in a liberal arts education. Examples of the classicist approach to teaching are Adler and Hutchins' Great Books Program (Hutchins, 1952) and Adler's Paidea Proposal, a proposal for reforming schools by requiring all students to take the same course of study for twelve years (Adler, 1993).

In the classicist classroom, not only must the students know content, but they must experience the process of acquiring knowledge that is characteristic of that content area. Each form of content knowledge has a logical structure of its own. The classicist feels that knowledge must be learned in a form that reflects the content itself. For example:

Science - dispassion and detachment

Literature - passion and involvement

Art or Music - encouragement of creative expression

The teacher serves as a model to students in several ways. Teachers must portray "the virtues of reason, open-mindedness, regard for evidence, intellectual curiosity, reflective habit of mind, and judicious skepticism" (Fenstermacher & Soltis, 1986, p. 40). Values are taught through the investigation of the specific content one teaches. In practice, the intellectual manner is part of the content.

In this approach, the teacher prepares extensively for lessons and adds to the basic content by including supplemental texts, visual aids, teacher-made materials, etc. The classicist teacher is confident that the content holds great interest and value for the student. Such teachers want to bring the subject matter alive using the most stimulating methods they can imagine.

Students are expected to show moral strength and integrity as they reach the goal of intellectual freedom. Through acquiring intellectual values and content, students will be freed from dogma, convention and stereotype. They are released from learning unimportant facts and mundane skills. The goal of the teacher as classicist is to assure that students develop academic and scholarly minds (Davis, 1982).

The classroom environment reflects the essence of the values of the particular content area. For example, the room of the classicist art teacher would be highly creative—possibly filled with a tremendous variety of materials, work tables, displays of student work, etc. Or the classroom of an enthusiastic social studies teacher, who has become a Civil War "historian," may well contain 15 boxes of Civil War memorabilia.

Hard work and fair-mindedness are highly valued in this approach because it is only by vigor and high standards that one can be free. The teacher's job is to focus upon content and arrange for students to confront the subject matter in the way the specialist in the field experiences it.

Classicist

<u>Teacher</u> as expert and source of inspiration

<u>Student</u> as scholar/citizen

<u>Environment</u> appropriate to specific subject area content

<u>Focus</u> on specific subject area content

<u>Emphasis</u> on CONTENT and CRITIQUE

The authors have broadened the approaches to teaching to include a fourth, technological orientation. The characteristics and principles that define this approach are markedly distinct from the previous three approaches. As the name suggests, information *per se* holds a central position of importance. Information in general identifies the information age. However, in this approach to teaching, *information is distinct from knowledge.* Also, interpreting information and its acquisition and management are different from teaching the substance of a particular subject area.

In identifying and naming the teacher as "Informationist," it is important to note that it is an emerging approach, with an emphasis on a changing world and a number of changing and expanding roles. For example, the recognition that the vastness of information available precludes any single teacher from "knowing it all" drastically changes the role of the teacher. *The teacher's role is redefined as that of an interpreter.* As such, teachers assist students to re-think the role of information... to judge, sift, expand or delete information. In so doing, the

The Informationist Approach (an emerging orientation)

teacher models how information could be valued and discusses the moral dimensions and responsibility of acquired knowledge. The teacher is responsible for helping students evaluate and derive meaning from the uncensored availability of information.

The role of the student is expanded in several ways. Students are connected to vast amounts of information. They are not "given" information (executive), nor guided (humanist), nor inspired to experience certain forms of knowledge (classicist). Rather, information is "out there" for the taking. As students become proficient in exploring and learning information by themselves from their computers, it is often a student who informs the teacher! Learner and teacher can occasionally reverse roles and/or become participants who hold parallel roles. Also, because they are connected via computer to the World Wide Web, students become part of a global community as well as a classroom community.

As you might expect, *the environment is filled with technological equipment.* The informationist classroom, however, which contains numbers of on-line computers and various types of printers, differs from an executive setting that may *happen* to have terminals which are primarily used to work through programmed materials. Informationist classrooms are rich with materials for students to use for desktop publishing, making presentations and creating visual aids.

The authors suggest that the informationist is an approach born of the post-modern era which holds that knowledge is ever changing (Doll, Jr., 1993a, MacDonald, 1995, see also Slattery, 1995a, 1995b). Without the constancy of knowledge (executive), a shift or change in orientation may have to be recognized. Nowhere in the philosophy of education is the opportunity for "global perspectives" more obvious (Slattery, 1995a), and nowhere in writing about the role of the teacher is it more evident that *teacher as interpreter* is an acknowledgment of the need to find meaning in information.

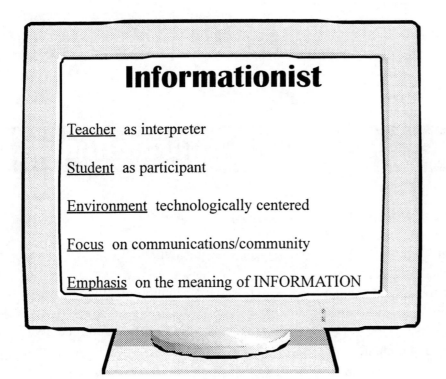

Informationist

Teacher as interpreter

Student as participant

Environment technologically centered

Focus on communications/community

Emphasis on the meaning of INFORMATION

Basic Tenets

Executive

<u>Teacher</u> as manager

<u>Student</u> as consumer

<u>Environment</u> task oriented

<u>Focus</u> on the end product

<u>Emphasis</u> on the role of TEACHER

Humanist

<u>Teacher</u> as facilitator

<u>Student</u> as self-directed learner

<u>Environment</u> rich with multiple resources for students

<u>Focus</u> on self-actualization and exploration

<u>Emphasis</u> on the role of LEARNER

Classicist

<u>Teacher</u> as expert and source of inspiration

<u>Student</u> as scholar/citizen

<u>Environment</u> appropriate to specific subject area content

<u>Focus</u> on specific subject area content

<u>Emphasis</u> on CONTENT and CRITIQUE

Informationist

<u>Teacher</u> as interpreter

<u>Student</u> as participant

<u>Environment</u> technologically centered

<u>Focus</u> on communications/community

<u>Emphasis</u> on the meaning of INFORMATION

Exercises

◆ Instructional Orientation Profile   16

◆ Example Philosophy Statements   17

◆ Philosophy Reflected in Educational
   Practices and Classroom Activities   20

◆ Philosophy Reflected in Policy Making   23
   Grading Policies   23
   Discipline Policies   26

INSTRUCTIONAL ORIENTATION PROFILE

Describe your style. Each box below contains descriptive phrases or words. Score each group of words, giving yourself (4) for the descriptors most like you, (3) for the next, (2) for the next and (1) for the least like you. (**Score across each category**.) Next, add scores in each column (down) to obtain column totals.

CLASSROOM ENVIRONMENT	◆ Task-oriented ◆ Organized / Efficient / Structured ◆ Commercially prepared material	◆ Student-oriented ◆ Flexible – Spontaneous activity ◆ Student-generated material	◆ Content-oriented ◆ Goal-directed / Semi-structured ◆ Teacher-prepared material	◆ Technology-oriented ◆ Production-dominated activity ◆ Materials created on computer
LESSON PLANS	◆ Specific objectives are clearly defined ◆ Essential elements of instruction are addressed ◆ Meets district guidelines and scope and sequence	◆ Long-term, broadly structured outcomes ◆ Thematic units and integrated curriculum ◆ Student choice of what to learn	◆ Emphasis on depth of knowledge ◆ Instruction extends beyond district guidelines ◆ Extensive resources (field trips, outside speakers)	◆ Open ended ◆ Multi-level inquiry planning (spiral) ◆ Lessons emphasize technological skills and information interpreting techniques
DISCIPLINE	◆ Teacher / School-developed rules ◆ Positive reinforcement for desired behaviors ◆ Defined consistent consequences for undesired behaviors	◆ Classroom community meetings to discuss choices and consequences ◆ Rules established cooperatively by teacher and students ◆ Serious problems dealt with on individual contract basis	◆ Teacher models desired behavior ◆ Each student is responsible for his or her own conduct ◆ Focuses on ethics and moral development	◆ Community responsibility is stressed ◆ Teachers and students dialogue to clarify expectations ◆ Procedures govern student interaction with technology
ACTIVITIES	◆ Independent / Seat work ◆ Lecture–Direct instruction ◆ Daily or weekly homework assignments/projects	◆ Dialogue Journaling ◆ Cooperative learning ◆ Student-chosen activities and projects	◆ In-depth research on topics ◆ Lecture/discussion questions ◆ Extensive reading	◆ Students working at on-line terminals ◆ Peer teaching ◆ Students create presentations and projects
GRADING/ EVALUATIONS	◆ End-of-Unit mastery testing ◆ Progress measured objectively and frequently ◆ Tests assess stated objectives	◆ Ongoing portfolio assessment ◆ Graded for effort as well as achievement ◆ Self and peers evaluate process as well as product	◆ Essay and objective tests ◆ Graded on ability to apply knowledge ◆ High standards	◆ Student work graded on decision making, diversity of resources used, and style and completeness ◆ Students are also evaluated on technical competence ◆ Feedback is often given via E-mail
KNOWLEDGE/ INSTRUCTION	◆ Logical step-by-step instruction ◆ Drill and practice focused on specific outcome ◆ Focus on mastering the basic/essential skills	◆ "First-hand" experiences/discovery ◆ Manipulation / experimentation ◆ Students construct their own meaning / develop personal understanding	◆ Intense study and immersion in content ◆ Teacher transmission ◆ Depth of knowledge is goal	◆ Students are taught to search for information ◆ Open exploration / student interest ◆ Interpretation of meaning emphasized
TEACHER'S ROLE	◆ Manager ◆ Organizer ◆ Planner	◆ Facilitator ◆ Explorer ◆ Co-learner	◆ Expert ◆ Mentor ◆ Guide	◆ Interpreter ◆ Consultant ◆ Connector
	COLUMN TOTAL	**COLUMN TOTAL**	**COLUMN TOTAL**	**COLUMN TOTAL**

EXAMPLE PHILOSOPHY STATEMENTS

Read the following examples and decide which of the four philosophical approaches each most clearly represents. Use a highlighter to identify supporting sentences, phrases or key words that influenced your decision. (If possible, discuss your supporting arguments with a classmate.)

John

As a child develops and matures, many of life's important lessons and facts about the world are learned naturally, without overt or deliberate effort. I feel it is my job as a teacher to take that natural child and show him/her how to stretch both mind and abilities to reach higher levels.

There are many opportunities in the social studies field to challenge students' minds. By reflecting upon the successes and failure of past civilizations, students can be shown the value of an open mind as well as the importance of supporting statements and evidence when debating an issue. Students can be taught the value of developing healthy skepticism when evaluating someone's ideas. Students need to be taught the skills of reading critically, researching a topic and accurately reporting their findings. I believe students will rise to the level of performance that we as teachers present as attainable.

The opportunity to work with students challenges me every day to do my very best. I, in return, show my students respect for their efforts to do their best. I am confident that the answer to improving our society depends upon the ability of our schools to truly prepare the future leaders of our country. It is my hope to contribute to this process.

Basic Philosophic Approach: _____

Carol

Children are our future's most precious resource. They are the ones who will inherit the promises and problems the world has to offer. As a teacher, I will foster academic and cognitive growth without sacrificing individuality by providing children with the tools necessary for success. I have high expectations because I want each child in my class to be all that he/she can possibly be. I will provide them with a safe environment where they'll be free to take risks and make choices without fear of failure. Part of this will be accomplished through joint goal-setting and individual contracting. My students will take an active role in their academic growth.

Parents play a key role in the success of their child's learning. It is my belief that parents need to be actively involved in their child's education. I will do my best to keep the lines of communication open to accomplish this and work as a team with the parent and child. This may include weekly phone calls, letters home, and parent conferences.

Basic Philosophic Approach: _____

Mark

I am excited about the educational opportunities in today's world. Thanks to technology not only has the world become smaller through instant communications and networks, but also, individuals have a real chance for equality. Historically, either age, gender, race, geographic location or levels of education held people to pre-established roles. Access to worldwide technology access opens doors equally to all potential learners.

I view my future role as an educator to be a very important one. I feel an obligation to help my students to learn how to use their wonderful opportunities and to help them to be able to evaluate the veracity of information that they discover. It will be equally important to consult with students about the unethical misuse of technologies.

I also feel it is important to build a sense of social cooperation among my students. Students can learn from one another and share information for the betterment of all class members.

Basic Philosophic Approach: _____

Sarah

I see teaching as the most important contribution I can make to the future of our nation's youth. The classroom is a very exciting and yet demanding environment. Teaching offers me a challenge; one that I am very pleased to have a chance to meet! I believe that the mission of educators today is to produce knowledgeable adults who can function well in our evolving culture. To meet this challenge, each of us must demand much of ourselves as teachers.

Teachers should be accountable for the learning that takes place in their classrooms. I believe in outcome-based education. To achieve the maximum results, I like to use a variety of strategies and methods in order to reach all the learning styles of my students. Both daily and long-term lesson planning are crucial to making sure student needs are met. I am a very organized person who values efficiency in myself and others. Teachers can work together to plan for reaching every student. As a junior high teacher, I have seen the tremendous demand put on students to master each content area and I feel strongly that students need to be taught study skills and test strategies in order to feel more successful.

I see motivation as the key to helping students achieve. I think assignments and practice homework should be meaningful to the students... relevance is motivating to the learner. School should be an exciting place to come each day and I feel that I can provide students with the motivation to want to attend school.

Basic Philosophic Approach: _____

(For answers, see Answer Key p. 45)

REVIEW EXERCISE: BASIC TENETS

List five basic tenets of the philosophical approaches of the Executive, Humanist, Classicist, and Informationist.

EXECUTIVE:
1. Teacher as _____

2. Student as _____

3. Environment _____

4. Focus _____

5. Emphasis _____

HUMANIST:
1. Teacher as _____

2. Student as _____

3. Environment _____

4. Focus _____

5. Emphasis _____

CLASSICIST:
1. Teacher as _____

2. Student as _____

3. Environment _____

4. Focus _____

5. Emphasis _____

INFORMATIONIST:
1. Teacher as _____

2. Student as _____

3. Environment _____

4. Focus _____

5. Emphasis _____

PHILOSOPHY REFLECTED IN EDUCATIONAL PRACTICES AND CLASSROOM ACTIVITIES

The way you conceptualize your teaching role, the type of student you hope to develop, and the envronment you create to achieve your goals intersect to create your own personal belief system. That system, whether consciously or unconsciously, guides everything you do as a teacher. The emphasis you give to each of these areas as you combine them and begin working with students makes you, in a very real sense, unique!

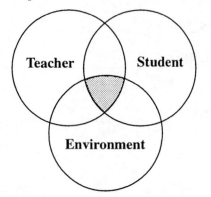

EDUCATIONAL PRACTICES AND CLASSROOM ACTIVITIES:

Educational practices are the policies or programs you use every day in your classroom. Examples of educational practices include:

◆ Use of learning centers
◆ Use of lecture as the primary method of instruction
◆ Grading students only against their own progress
◆ Recording student "Time on Task"
◆ Use of computers

Classroom activities, on the other hand, include exercises and procedures that may be expressions of a practice. Examples of classroom activities that are used on a regular basis in the classroom might include:

◆ Use of repetitive practice or drill
◆ Use of peer coaching
◆ Charting of student progress on wall charts
◆ Note-taking during lectures
◆ E-mail communication

EXERCISE:

Make a list of practices and activities that might be commonly observed in a typical elementary, middle school or high school class. You do not need to be concerned with whether something is technically a practice or an activity. Brainstorm (as quickly as you can) as many ideas as possible about what you see happening in classes today. Record your ideas below. (See Answer Key p. 45 for possible ideas).

Practices and Activities:

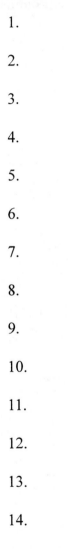

1.

2.

3.

4.

5.

6.

7.

8.

9.

10.

11.

12.

13.

14.

EXERCISE: EDUCATIONAL PRACTICES AND ACTIVITIES

Look at each educational practice or classroom activity listed below and decide which approach it most accurately reflects. Place each statement under the proper category.

Note: There may be some that could fit in several categories. Also, some categories may have less than five.

- ◆ **Teacher** assigns partners and teams for group work.
- ◆ Standardized content is often presented in programmed study guides and/or outlines.
- ◆ Frequent use of cooperative learning.
- ◆ Learning is global and communication is virtually instantaneous.
- ◆ Helps students realize that "knowledge is power."
- ◆ Uses thematic units/integrated curriculum.
- ◆ Questions and dialogue often occur via e-mail between students and teacher.
- ◆ Students take notes and/or respond to discussion questions.
- ◆ Self and peer evaluation is common.
- ◆ Instruction frequently follows a lockstep format with all students.
- ◆ Room is production oriented.
- ◆ Computers are on-line
- ◆ Student skill mastery is goal with opportunities for remediation and retesting.
- ◆ Is comfortable working in multi-age classrooms.
- ◆ Stresses liberal arts curriculum.
- ◆ Teacher shows respect for gathering evidence and for people who argue well.
- ◆ Learning centers are crucial to provide optimum choice.
- ◆ Peer teaching is common.

Executive	Humanist	Classicist	Informationist
1.	1.	1.	1.
2.	2.	2.	2.
3.	3.	3.	3.
4.	4.	4.	4.
5.	5.	5.	5.

PHILOSOPHY REFLECTED IN POLICY MAKING

Having reviewed four different philosophical approaches to teaching and how these belief structures influence a teacher's choice of methods, practices and activities, you may still wonder why knowing this information will be important to you. Beyond helping you to define your own philosophy, how can this information help you? It will help you to know where other teachers are "coming from!" In addition to being an individual classroom teacher, you are also going to be a member of a teaching staff. You may also be a member of a specific high school department, or a member of a team teaching pair. So, you will constantly need to relate to your colleagues. As stated in the introduction, philosophical beliefs are at the base of everything you do as a teacher... everything goes back to philosophy! For example, look at both grading and discipline policies.

GRADING POLICIES

The following scenario shows how four different teachers (holding four distinctly different philosophies) have created conflicting policies regarding grading. Each policy makes perfect sense to that teacher. Each teacher can easily create a great defense for the policy he or she has chosen. Good staff relationships, however, are not built upon making great defenses! Cooperation and a willingness to understand those you work with will be the foundations of good staff relations. Read the descriptions that follow the scenario below and decide which philosophy is held by each teacher and why. (See Answer Key).

At Carrington Middle School, Julia Dawson is the team leader of the Language Arts Department. Carrington is an inner city school serving an ethnically diverse and multilingual population. Because of its high needs population, the school was "adopted" by a consortium of businesses and industries that are located within its attendance boundaries. Additionally, because there is a very active and exceptional after school program housed at Carrington, many families of the local business people choose to send their children to Carrington.

There are four instructors who teach language arts/communications. Julia has been at Carrington for nine years and is the senior member of the English faculty. Doug Martin previously a high school English literature teacher, has worked at Carrington Middle School for six years and is three years away from retirement. Claire Hilliker was hired right after completing her student teaching with Mr. Whitworth and is the newest member of the faculty. Mr. Whitworth had been transferred from Desmond Middle School two years ago after five years in the district.

All Carrington faculty are charged with reviewing grading policies practiced within their disciplines. Karen Englehart, the principal, has encouraged open dialogue among faculty and staff to help determine the future direction of the school. Although the site-based, shared decision making process Karen initiated is working well with regard to many school issues, faculty are just beginning their discussions about why they grade students as they do. Julia, as the team leader, began the dialogue with her team members.

Julia Dawson understands most of her students' capabilities, because she devotes much time and effort to getting to know each of her students as individuals. She makes frequent modifications and adaptations of classwork to accommodate the individual needs and many "extenuating circumstances" of her students. Sometimes students take advantage of Julia's understanding nature; however, even knowing that, she believes strongly that her approach is best for kids. Julia is one of two Language Arts teachers of the eighth grade team who is ESL certified. Therefore, she has some students with limited English proficiency. Julia not only allows students' writing assignments to be in their primary language, she encourages it for certain types of assignments, such as poetry. Although she marks papers with corrective feedback, she never assigns grades per se. Her comments instruct students on how to improve and correct their work, and she allows her students to resubmit any paper multiple times until they are pleased with the work. Because the district requires grades, she gives most of her students A's, and reserves B's primarily for those whose effort is lacking.

Philosophic Approach: _____

Why?

Because Doug Martin's students are taught how to produce research papers that require rigorous effort, many parents who have high aspirations for their children's future college education are anxious to place their children in Mr. Martin's class. Doug Martin is either revered and loved by his students, or is revered and feared. Doug knows his subject so well that students are quite in awe of his vast knowledge. His command of literary history, as well as of contemporary writers, is recognized throughout the community. Mr. Martin and his current flock of earnest students participate in every literary event in the local area. It is clearly understood by parents and students alike, that part of a student's grade depends on credit earned for a) attendance at, and critiques of, a community play, b) participation in at least one round-table book discussion group, and c) independent reports. All work is graded only on merit, not effort. Doug's enthusiasm for his subject inspires many students to want to read more extensively and to rise to his high expectations for writing. Quality-based grading has become the norm and students know that any work that does not meet that high standard will be graded harshly.

Philosophic Approach: _____

Why?

Although new to teaching, Claire Hilliker is not new to instruction using computers. She had worked for several years at a large software company in their training department before becoming a teacher. The principal, recognizing Claire's expertise, put her in charge of upgrading the computer on-line services at the school. Claire's classroom is a hub of activity not only for her students, but also for other teachers who come to Claire and her now well-trained students for help. Claire assigns work projects for students to learn about period writers such as the Harlem Renaissance writers they are studying now. Students have been instructed in the use of a wide variety of resources to inform them, and Claire gives higher grades to student reports that show such exploration and utilization of resources. The same letter grade is assigned to all members of the group for group reports. With help from Claire, students monitor themselves and group members assure that the work load is fair. However, not all her students enjoy working with others. Some find that immersion in books and stories is as enjoyable as the fact finding and, after a preliminary computer search, can be found in the library corner of Claire's room just reading. These students use the computer only to type. Other students never leave their computer, but also work alone. So, although Claire gives a certain number of points for group participation, these students are still able to receive high grades if they produce superior work.

Philosophic Approach: _____

Why?

It seems that Mr. Whitworth is always at school! He arrives by 7:00 in the morning and can usually be found in his classroom until 7 or 8:00 in the evening. Students know that they can come to his room after school and he'll happily put them to work helping him. He is always friendly and open and appreciative for their help. He grades all students' daily work, records their grades and places their critiqued work in file folders for the next day… before he leaves. Mr. Whitworth has high expectations for his students' work. For example, when he recently assigned research papers, he was careful to show everyone exactly what he expected. He showed model papers from past students and taught them how to use a rubric of written expectations of the paper's content to check their own writing. He communicated his expectations to parents as well and sent home a "weekly countdown" and progress report so that all student would be sure to have their work turned in on time. Although he always set firm performance guidelines for all work assigned in his class, he also took great care to grade on the curve because he was concerned about being fair to each student. Mr. Whitworth recently obtained his ESL certification in order to learn methods that will allow him to know how to be fair to all students, given the vast differences in their ability to achieve a given task.

Philosophic Approach: _____

Why?

DISCIPLINE POLICIES

Your approach to classroom management and discipline is a reflection of your underlying philosophy of education. The following information describes six behavior management approaches. One of these approaches will fit a particular philosophy better than another. After reading each paragraph, decide which philosophy would most likely match each approach/technique. (See Answer Key p. 45)

I. Behaviorist Approach – Behavior Modification (Skinner, 1968)

The teacher believes that student behaviors are a complex set of responses that have been conditioned by his/her environment. Those behaviors that are followed by rewards are more likely to be repeated than behaviors that are not. In addition, behaviors that are followed by punishment are less likely to recur.

This behavior approach recommends that the teacher:

1. Provide positive reinforcers to increase the probability for on-task behaviors.
2. Provide punishment or negative reinforcers to teach students to substitute off-task with on-task behaviors.

Best Philosophic Match: _____

II. Assertive Discipline Approach (Canter, 1992).

Discipline is the responsibility of the teacher. This assertive approach is a rules-based approach with external controls. The teacher takes charge of his/her own classroom. The teacher's response style is open, direct and predetermined. The focus is on students acting in a way that the instructor finds desirable.

The assertive discipline approach recommends that the teacher:

1. Specify exact behaviors required and those not tolerated.
2. Develop and follow a plan for encouraging and guiding student toward choosing appropriate behaviors.
3. Use positive reinforcement as a preventive technique.
4. Use redirecting techniques before using minimal consequences for inappropriate behaviors.
5. Develop a monitoring system that tracks students' behaviors.
6. Seek and expect parent and administrative support.

Best Philosophic Match: _____

III. Cooperation Through Communication Approach (Ginott, 1971)

The teacher believes that language greatly influences how students view themselves. Likewise, teachers' verbal and non-verbal interactions facilitate students' willingness to cooperate.

The Ginott approach recommends that the teacher:

1. Develop a descriptive, non judgmental language style when communicating with students.
    (a) Avoid power struggles that lead to resentment.
    (b) Avoid using any kind label (e.g., "poor reader," "fast reader," "good").
2. Carefully select what to say and when to say it; utilize body language, utilize active listening techniques, and supportive replies.
3. Model businesslike attitude; avoid communicating unintended messages to students.
4. Emphasize each person's responsibility for his/her own conduct.
5. Emphasize formative, rather than summative, evaluation when communicating with students/parents.
6. Develop a level of professionalism that underscores student trust and confidence in the teacher.

Best Philosophic Match: _____

IV. Rational Choices Approach (Glasser, 1986)

The teacher assumes that students are rational beings and capable of choosing to cooperate and be on-task.

The rational approach recommends that the teacher:

1. Lead students in classroom meetings and conduct one-to-one conferences to help students focus and analyze their choices of behaviors.
2. Teachers and students cooperatively establish rules for behavior expectations.
3. Enforce these rules strictly; use both desirable and undesirable consequences for behavior choices.

Best Philosophic Match: _____

V. Ethical Approach (Schwartz & Bilsky, 1987)

This approach helps children learn ethical behavior which will be the basis of judgment about action in the school at all times and should apply in their lives outside of school. Its focus is on shaping moral character to help children make choices to live a good (ethical) life.

Students are taught that certain things are wrong and should be avoided for that reason. Students learn that there is a rule against X because X is wrong and they are helped to understand why it is so. (Example: Children should be taught not to steal because it is wrong.)

The teacher uses language to develop sense of ethics (voice of conscience). Children learn to think, talk and act morally (children learn a sense of right and wrong). Internal voice is shaped by external language.

The ethical approach recommends that the teacher:

1. Model ethical behavior and clarify processes used in determining such ethical responses.
2. Use parables/stories/examples to illustrate moral choices.
3. Teach strategies of higher-order thinking.

Best Philosophic Match: _____

VI. Group Process (Kohn, 1997)

This approach emphasizes creating caring communities in the school/classroom. It promotes compassion and responsibility. It assumes that competition controlled by rewards or "consequences" is inherently destructive. The teacher helps children make decisions about their behavior. For example, the teacher provides opportunities for decision-making by helping children to take another's point of view, by holding class meetings so children can make classroom decisions, and by encouraging empathy, eliminating classroom competition and using literature to foster good values.

The group process approach recommends that the teacher:

1. Hold frequent class meetings where problems are resolved through discussion, reflection and cooperative effort.
2. Support students in role-play strategies for taking another person's point of view.

Best Philosophic Match: _____

Creating
Your Philosophy of Education Statement

◆ How to Write Your Statement   30

◆ Using Your Philosophy Statement
in a Job Interview   37

How to Write Your Statement

The process of writing a statement of philosophy can begin with creating a simple inventory of your likes and dislikes from your own personal history. The process will lead to a narrative or story about what you currently believe teaching is about. Those who read your final statement will be interested in the sound and "feel" of what you have to say, as well as the content or issues you address.

Note: ***DO NOT*** *include the labels of the philosophical orientations (i.e., executive, informationist) in your narrative statement. These labels are only descriptors that aid in discussion of important concepts, but have little relevance to someone else reading your teaching application.*

Reflecting On Your Own History

Sometimes exploring your own background gives you insight into your philosophy of education. As you read each question, jot down some notes about your thoughts. Discuss your answers with a friend or colleague.

1. Where did you grow up, attend school (including college)?

2. What educational background did your parents have, and what type of job did they have?

3. What were each of the schools like when you attended?

4. What were some of the significant memories, events, teachers and subject matter from these schools?

5. Who was most influential in your decision to become a teacher? Why?

6. What skills that are most important for a teacher to develop?

7. What is the role of education today? Where do you differ with the "predominant" role, or is there one?

Note: These questions ***are not*** *intended for your final written statement. They are only meant to guide your thinking.*

NEXT...

◆ Using the space provided on the following page, create a list, like a "to do" list, of practices, activities and events that you enjoy most as a teacher. Place what you like most in one column (example: water play, story time, choir or band).

◆ Add to this list the practices, activities and events you liked as a student (example: extended time for reading, independent math practice, clay and painting).

◆ Now, list those practices, activities and events that you like least as a teacher (example: lots of paperwork, re-teaching, being a disciplinarian).

◆ Finally, list those practices, activities and events that you liked least as a student (example: repetitive practice, lots of paperwork, long sit time, surprise or pop quizzes).

Like Most	**Like Least**
As teacher:	As teacher:
As student:	As student:

Now, go back to the **Instructional Orientation Profile** on page 16 and create a list from each subscale by identifying those ideas you like most. Begin with "Classroom Environment" and proceed in the same manner through all seven subscales.

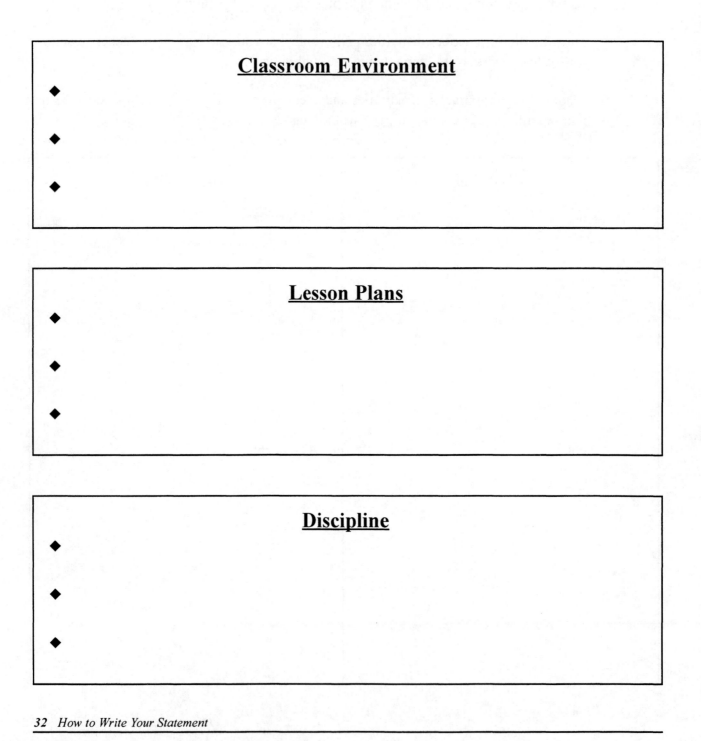

Classroom Environment

◆

◆

◆

Lesson Plans

◆

◆

◆

Discipline

◆

◆

◆

Activities

◆

◆

◆

Grading/Evaluations

◆

◆

◆

Knowledge/Instruction

◆

◆

◆

Teacher's Role

◆

◆

◆

USING YOUR LIST TO WRITE YOUR STATEMENT

In order to translate your list of preferences into sentences for your statement, you may wish to try one, or both, of the following methods:

Method One: Chunking

Group sections of the subscale that appear to go together (i.e., Classroom Environment and Activities). Create several sentences from ideas on the combined lists that describe and summarize this aspect of your philosophy.

Example 1)   I like a classroom that is quiet. When students have an ordered place to read and think, they can finish their tasks quickly.

Example 2)   I like an active classroom where students work in small groups to explore the topic we are studying. In order to help in this exploration I will have materials that encourage not only reading (magazines, books, computer programs, newspapers), but also art, music and physical movement.

Method Two: Belief Statements

An alternate approach to start the narrative process is to write sentences that make complete "I believe" statements.
   ◆ I believe that the goal of education is...
   ◆ I believe that the role of the teacher is...
   ◆ I believe that students should...
   ◆ I believe that parents...

Now begin to combine your thoughts into paragraph form. Consider the following **strategies for writing clear statements;**
   ◆ Use the active voice. Write *I believe* instead of ... *the beliefs I have are...*
   ◆ Use the present, not passive, tense. Write I *believe*, instead of *I have believed.*
   ◆ Use a confident and firm tone, not a tentative or aggressive one.
   ◆ Use action words whenever possible. Following is a list of action words you might consider:

accomplish	document	implement	organize	stimulate
activate	engage	improve	plan	strengthen
advise	establish	install	prepare	structure
change	expand	instigate	present	supply
communicate	function as	join	promote	support
construct	generate	measure	review	validate
create	help	monitor	revise	write
delegate				

*Excerpt from Better Resumes for Sales & Marketing Personnel, 1993

SAMPLE STATEMENTS

The following samples show how several students have written their philosophy of education statement. One sample is provided for each of the four orientations.

Sample of Executive

THE GOAL OF EDUCATION TODAY

I think the goal of education should be to prepare students to be successful, contributing members of society. Students need to be provided with opportunities to learn all the skills needed to fulfill their potential. Educators who set up classrooms that are learning, probing, seeking centers allow students these opportunities. Many times, curriculum guidelines tend to push teachers to "move along" regardless of the mastery level of their students. I think teachers need to choose carefully the content and skills-mastery they focus on.

Sometimes schools and teachers have their focus on "crowd control" rather than on learning. Unfortunately, there are some students who have not been raised by their parents to value an education as the gift that it is. These students present a challenge. Teachers need to motivate them, give them goals to attain and provide the praise needed to keep students on track.

It is my responsibility as the teacher to make the learning environment one where each student can succeed at a mastery level and show academic growth. By varying my methods, I believe that I can teach all my students the skills they need to contribute to our society.

Sample of Humanist

MY PHILOSOPHY STATEMENT

Every student can learn and can be successful. It is my job as an educator to determine how each student is able to acquire knowledge and then to provide varied opportunities for each student to learn. Education must advance the dignity, self-esteem, growth and integrity of all students as individuals. By providing a positive, caring environment in the classroom, I hope to give students a start on a successful school experience.

I am a kind and caring individual. My classroom will be a good place to be. I will happily give my time and talents to help a student be successful. I am fair and reasonable in my expectations of students. I am honest and genuine in my interactions with students and fellow teachers. Perseverance and self-motivation are my strong points... along with a good sense of humor to keep me going. I am the mother of three children, and have 17 years of experience in nurturing. This experience has been a tremendous asset to me as I work with students.

I plan to use the interest and prior knowledge of my students in determining the direction of many of my instructional thematic units. I believe that students should be self-directed and responsible for their learning; however, I want to foster cooperation between students as well. To do this I think cooperative learning groups and class meetings are helpful.

I want to have an opportunity to help students grow to be healthy and successful so that they can feel more content in our fast paced society.

"The students had memorized everything, but they didn't know what anything meant."

The above quotation, by the theoretical physicist and science educator Richard Feyman, unfortunately is an apt description of what all too often is the outcome of science education in our secondary schools. In this case, Dr. Feyman was describing students at a school where he was guest lecturing. The students knew the complex equations describing the polarization of light, but were unable to recognize the phenomenon when it occurred before their very eyes.

As we approach the 21st century, we face issues in science that are staggering in their complexity. Among these are: fulfilling the energy demand of our technologically-dependent society, preserving the environment and meeting the food-supply demands of an ever-increasing world population. It is essential that the high school students of today become scientifically literate in order to meet these challenges and provide leadership in solving these problems in the future.

While learning the language and explanations of the major concepts themselves are certainly important, I believe that critical concepts are best learned and retained by students in an experiential forum, i.e., an inquiry-based approach in the high school science laboratory. My classroom will "come alive" as a place to both discover and to practice scientific inquiry. Science is an active discipline that requires students "to do science," not to sit passively while receiving a lecture "about science."

Sample of Informationist

MY VIEW OF EDUCATION

I believe that the role of the teacher in the emerging 21st century is to help students understand that our world is extended to a world community and that learning and information is rapidly changing. As a teacher I hope to support students as they communicate with each other and use the knowledge they gain through technology in a responsible manner. As a teacher who feels connected to students as they explore technology, I also hope to learn from my students.

My classroom environment will reflect many tools that allow for cooperation and exploration. For example, I would promote the use of computer terminals, peer teaching and partnering, multi-age classrooms, and multi-media reporting styles. Questioning and dialogue, along with clarification, are techniques that will help me support this exploration.

As I work with students, I hope they gain experience in working with the changing roles of people and the multiple and expanding roles of information.

USING YOUR PHILOSOPHY STATEMENT
IN A JOB INTERVIEW

In addition to completing your job application (which includes your written philosophy statement), you will also be interviewed by principals who will undoubtedly ask you questions abut your philosophy. It is helpful, therefore, to consider the kinds of questions that can be generated from a philosophy statement.

Consider creating responses not only to general questions regarding your roles and responsibilities, but also to the specific ways you would implement educational practices that are consistent with your philosophy. Think about the following specifics. As you work through these concepts, jot down key ideas and phrases.

◆ behavior objectives/outcomes

◆ discipline/classroom management

◆ creating a leaning environment

◆ grading

◆ lesson plans

◆ homework

◆ learning styles of students

◆ curriculum

◆ parent-teacher relationships

◆ teaching methods

Practice Exercise #1 – How Will You Implement Your Philosophy?

> Write a brief response to the following questions that could be asked by a personnel director in an interview. Use the space provided to prepare your response. (A sample of what a typical "Executive style" response could be is provided in the Answer Key p. 46)

1. **Interviewer:** How will you arrange your classroom environment to accomplish your teaching goals?

   Applicant:

2. **Interviewer:** How will you decide what to teach in a given subject area?

   Applicant:

3. **Interviewer:** Tell me about your homework policies.

   Applicant:

4. **Interviewer:** How do you plan to accommodate the different learning styles of your students?

   Applicant:

5. **Interviewer:** What kind of students are you trying to "create" through your teaching?

   Applicant:

Practice Exercise #2 – Your Follow-up Job Interview

> Write your responses to these additional questions. Note that several questions build on a prior answer or on your written statement of beliefs. (Samples of various possible responses are found in the Answer Key p. 46)

1. **Principal:** Describe your role as the teacher of this class.

   Applicant:

2. **Principal:** You have described the role of the teacher. How would you describe your approach to classroom management?

   Applicant:

3. **Principal:** You have written about the goals of education today. What are some ways you can create an environment for achieving these goals?

   Applicant:

4. **Principal:** Describe your grading policy with respect to this class.

   Applicant:

5. **Principal:** When you create your lesson plans, what sources do you rely on?

   Applicant:

CONCLUSION

As you can see, your thought and work in **preparing your written philosophy of education statement** has accomplished more than simply the completion of an application form for employment. You should now be ready to **use the insights gained during this process** to interview more confidently, to secure a job and to better understand and communicate with other staff members.

In the past several years, there has been increased attention given to the importance of "the process" in learning. Hopefully, this workbook is one example of finding **real value** as a result of the process.

ABOUT THE AUTHORS

Jill Stamm (Ph.D. Learning and Instructional Technology) is a faculty associate for the Office of Professional Field Experiences in the College of Education at Arizona State University. She currently teaches the Assessment and Supervision of Instruction, a course for potential mentor teachers who work with a student teacher and/or a first year teacher. Jill is actively involved in research in both learning and cognition. Jill is also a placement liaison for seven school districts. Her research interests focus on brain development and in interpreting research to various groups, including teachers and parents.

Caroline R. Wactler (Ed.D. Secondary Education) is a faculty associate and student teacher supervisor for the Office of Professional Field Experiences in the College of Education at Arizona State University. She teaches mentors in the ASU Assessment and Supervision of Instruction course, teaches in ASU's Beginning Educator Support Team program, and places interns and students in four school districts. She is also a member of the research team at ASU's Professional Development School. Her research interests are in philosophy of education and democratic practice.

Appendix

HISTORICAL ROOTS OF THE EXECUTIVE APPROACH

The right of all people to be educated has become part of our American credo. Thomas Jefferson, often called the father of American education (Ravitch, 1984), drew a portion of his justification for mass education from the notion of fairness as well as the need to be educated for participation in the democratic process. The anthropological understanding of social order, particularly the individual's role in an organization is communicated in part in our education system (Feinberg & Soltis, 1992). Long before American authors wrote in support of the independent role of the learner however, historical figures such as Aristotle wrote about the status of the individual in society. He incorporated the ideal of empirical observation into his view of truth and knowledge, utilizing teaching techniques such as lectures and the written word (Smith, 1984). Aristotle found that human difference could be mediated by the interaction of nature and nurture. He supported the use of schools for the purpose of scientific exploration and achievement (Smith, 1984).

Taking charge from history, then, America in the 1900's set out to educate large numbers of students. In order to accommodate these numbers, the system that evolved (that of placing one teacher with a classroom of children of the same chronological age) was based on efficiency, not on learning principles. This formulation maintained itself because it was exactly that... efficient. The focus on efficiency, of doing more for less, is pervasive in this business-like, executive model of teaching. If learning is a transfer of knowledge from one source (teacher, textbook, programmed instruction) to another, the more knowledge you transfer to the most students using the fewest teachers... the better your system. The emergence of the behaviorist paradigm in psychology provided a learning theory to support this already emerging way of doing "business." B.F. Skinner (1968) advocated for programmed instruction in the schools. Behaviorism, based on the belief that learning is the observable outcome of a stimulus-response pairing that is reinforced, became the basis for education practice (Richelle, 1993). Skinner's work with laboratory animals encouraged him and others to conclude that learning is controllable and can be increased if the optimal contingency reinforcement schedule is maintained. Traditional schools across America began adopting programmed instructional materials, developed reward-based grading systems, and created discipline systems of reward and punishment contingencies.

Many of the techniques and instructional behaviors used by teachers every day in their classrooms have been extensively studied by researchers. Much of this research shows that the ways that teachers structure the learning environment and instructional tasks does, in fact, impact learning (Berliner, 1983; Hunter, 1971). This traditional executive approach is advocated by many community members and educators as an effective approach to the task of educating the American population.

HISTORICAL ROOTS OF THE HUMANIST APPROACH

Years of strict adherence to behaviorist principles left many psychologists and educators with both anecdotal and scientific evidence that conflicted with basic behaviorist doctrine. Mounting evidence showed that the *learner did play* a significant role in the learning process (Bousfield, 1953; Chomsky, 1959; Sachs, 1967; Anderson & Ortony, 1975). The simple stimulus-response paradigm cracked under the weight of such evidence. Cognitive psychology developed to examine and explain the significance of the individual in learning. The importance of prior knowledge and context was established by researchers experimentally and was widely reported in professional journals (Anderson & Ortony, 1975; Bransford & Johnson, 1972; Bransford, Barclay, & Franks, 1972). The significance of prior experience and context was also of great interest to anthropologists. Margaret Mead (1951) particularly charged American educators to study "the changing contexts of their students' socialization and upbringing in order to become better teachers" (Bogdan & Biklen, 1982, p.9). The groundwork was then prepared for psychologists such as Carl Rogers (1969, 1980) and Abraham Maslow to "popularize" notions of the interplay of experience and psychological states. Maslow wrote extensively about students' holistic needs, needs that are hierarchical as well as contextual (shown below) (Maslow, 1970).

Historically, the humanist paradigm was a challenge to societies controlled by social class and powerful government and church doctrine (Smith, 1984). During the late 18th century, philosophers and educators began to question the individual's right to express creative choice. The average man wanted control over his own destiny and several voices for *man* as *maker of meaning* emerged. Predominant among these voices are Pestalozzi and Froebel.

In 1799, Pestalozzi created a children's village, a school known as a *landmark or cradle* of today's elementary school (Downs, 1975). This school was a model used to teach poor children physically, morally and intellectually... a place to learn to live "self respecting" lives. Pestalozzi set out to demonstrate that children in need could recover and grow healthy in spirit. He advocated utilizing a continuum of methods from concrete to abstract, involving the learner through sensory observations, and recognizing learning and progress according to a child's own ability (Downs, 1975). By 1811, Fredrich Froebel had come in contact with Pestalozzi and he began his own school called the Child's Nurture and Activity Institute, later termed "the Kindergarten" (Lawerence, 1953). Froebel collected and published play materials, and nursery songs, and was lauded for the development of infant education.

Contemporary philosophy has been informed by the models of Froebel and Pestalozzi. A twentieth century leader of the University of Chicago's Laboratory School, John Dewey also wrote in support of the human ability to discover and implement independence of mind. In writing about the individual and participant/learner (Democracy in Education, 1964), Dewey demonstrated how a democracy required the creative input of all its' citizens. Dewey believed that we must educate the whole child. Using the scientific method (discovery learning) Dewey felt that educators can reshape education (Westbrook, 1991).

HISTORICAL ROOTS OF THE CLASSICIST APPROACH

The classicist approach to learning is perhaps the oldest historically. Whether it is utilizing the didactic methods of questioning and rhetoric stemming from the efforts of Socrates (399 B.C.), or current higher order thinking, the classicist paradigm is one of immersion in content and love of learning (Fenstermacher & Soltis, 1992). This is an approach to teaching that has often been aligned with the hierarchy evidenced in society itself. The opportunity to participate in reading, writing and "fair mindedness" was often reserved to males from the upper classes. It was rare, but not impossible, for females to participate in scholarly work (Smith, 1984).

The setting of a precedent for curriculum development in the direction of rigor and virtue resulted from the Greek experiences in the pre-Christian era. These events included an emphasis on individual commitment of judicious skepticism and inquiry. Socrates modeled such skepticism by holding meetings with his students and encouraging their questions and their inquiry as argument (Smith, 1984). Plato and Aristotle formalized this process by housing their students in academies where high standards and independence were fostered (Smith, 1984).

A common process for student thinking was known as scholasticism. This was a process by which the teacher and the students state a problem and then list arguments for and against a solution to a problem with a rational and logical analysis of each solution. Both brevity and clarity are virtues of scholasticism (Smith, 1984). One example of 13th century scholasticism is found in the work of St. Thomas Aquinas. He embodied and embraced the convictions of Christian theology and the need for human reasoning as facets of truth.

Mortimer Adler describes the abilities of higher order thinking in a manner related to a muscle. It is the exercise of this ability to think that allows the mind to reason and think clearly. Along with Robert Hutchins, Adler advocated the use of the Great Books of the Western World curriculum, a program that brought classic reading to many schools in 20th century America. The program was given much weight by 1930-1950 era educators, with reading, writing, and classic education a focus of schooling. By the 1960's, liberal education programs, such as the programs proposed by James B. Conant, were preparing thousands of high school students for an academic/university life (Ravitch, 1984). By the late 1970's the progressive movement of humanism returned, however, the scholarly emphasis of classicism is still considered the benchmark of rigor and attainment (Ravitch, 1984). As the teacher plans for scholarly work in contemporary schools, the practice of utilizing well known (perenialist) works contributed by both western Europe and the United States continues.

HISTORICAL ROOTS OF THE INFORMATIONIST APPROACH (an emerging orientation)

As we enter the 21st century, the informationist approach to teaching is emerging, as we have moved from the industrial age into the information age. This approach blends elements of both the content-based classicist approach with some of the features of the humanist or progressive approach. In reviewing this blend, it is important to note that strategies such as teacher/student in parallel assistantship and role reversal are housed in beliefs about shared systems of power. In investigating the historical roots of this approach that promote the teacher as student and student as teacher, one must begin with a contemporary review of writers of a post-modern integration of man and society.

Patrick Slattery (*Time and Education: Postmodern Eschatological Perspectives,* 1995) introduces the notion of time as "linear, hierarchical, and quantifiable" (p.3) that has been traditional in American schooling. For example, when educators think of the element of time, they typically measure and evaluate (the executive approach) how efficient someone has been with their time. Students are often asked: Have you finished yet? Did you get that in on time? Do you know when this is due? Or even, Who finished first? This type of structuring of time is typical in traditional classrooms. Time and learning in the informationist approach are understood instead as flexible and open. A paradigm of "past, present and future" is utilized as a way to think of time as it expands and is reconfigured for different classroom situations.

Slattery is not without understanding of the practicality of the teacher's world. He notes that the information age creates a dilemma for the executive model. With technology, we have the potential to allocate (or reallocate) time more efficiently. Vast amounts of information, in accessible form, compounds a problem for teachers, namely, how does a teacher think about all the information that *could* be gathered on a topic. Slattery wrote that school *curriculum should be viewed as flexible, and time as a resource*. He writes that time is the "flexible variable" in post-modern world, and the focus for schools should be on *how time is used* (Slattery, 1995).

A shift in curriculum for students may be a result of a shift in how we think about learners themselves. Doll (1993) reports that the expectations of the learner has shifted from classicism, or the learner's "mind as a muscle," to the production model of behaviorism, to the child control approach of the progressive movement. Doll writes that the labeling of the "mind" or "brain" must change in the post modernism of the information age. The traditional fixation on the brain as "thingness," to the brain as emergent and metamorphasizing changes the way that teachers view learners. As an informationist, the teacher views learners as information seekers, changing and sharing with their experience and that of others. It is the contention of Joseph Schwab and Donald Schoen, Doll writes, that the notion of brain as *verb* should replace the "moribund" notion of brain as *noun* (1993b).

Answer Key

pg. 17-18   John – Classicist; Carol – Humanist; Mark – Informationist; Sarah – Executive

pg. 19   *For answers, see page 14–Basic Tenets*

pg. 21

Executive	Humanist	Classicist	Informationist
1. Teaches study skills as part of the curriculum. 2. Uses specific behavioral objectives for each unit taught. 3. Often records students' "Time on Task." 4. Has students chart their individual progress on charts posted on the walls. 5. Stresses repetitive practice and drill.	1. Uses class meetings to discuss problems or concerns. 2. Students are graded against their own progress. 3. Students are graded for the effort they expend. 4. Students have partial or equal share in conducting parent conference. 5. Students help decide what they will study.	1. Units of study are presented in great depth. 2. Basic text is supplemented by additional library readings. 3. Reason, open-mindedness and intellectual curiosity are stressed. 4. Primarily uses lecture format. 5. Teacher shows great passion for the subject.	1. Individual academic counseling dominates the teacher's time. 2. Part of grade based on style and completeness of their presentations. 3. One student to one computer terminal is ideal ratio. 4. Part of grade is based on technical competence. 5. A focus is on learning to search for information.

pg. 22

Executive	Humanist	Classicist	Informationist
1. Teacher assigns *teams* partners and *trains* for group work.	1. Frequent use of cooperative learning.*	1. Helps students know "knowledge is power."*	1. Learning is global and communication is virtually instantaneous.
2. Standardized content is often presented in programmed study guides.	2. Uses thematic untils/integrated curriculum.	2. Student take notes and/or respond to discussion questions.**	2. Questions and dialogue often occur via e-mail between students and teacher.
3. Instruction frequently follows a lockstep format with all students.	3. Self and peer evaluation is common.*	3. Stresses liberal arts curriculum.	3. Room is production oriented.
4. Students mastery is goal with opportunities for remediation and retesting.	4. Is comfortable working in multi-age classrooms.*	4. Teacher shows respect for gathering evidence and for people who argue well.	4. Computers are on-line.
	5. Learning centers are crucial to provide optimum choice.		5. Peer teaching is common.

* *Could also appear under Informationist*
** *Could also appear under Executive*

pg. 24-25   Julia – Humanist; Doug – Classicist; Claire – Informationist; Mr. Whitworth – Executive

pg. 26-28   I. Executive; II. Executive; III. Informationist or Classicist; IV. Humanist; V. Classicist; VI. Humanist

pg. 38   The following are sample answers for **Practice Exercise #1**. The responses are written from the perspective of an "Executive style" applicant and are included to help give a "feel" for the kind of information one could include.

1. **Applicant:** I feel that the students should all be given jobs and responsibilities for keeping the classroom running smoothly. I will vary the seating arrangements often depending on the purpose of the activity we are doing. The room should be very well organized so that the materials are easy to find and kids know where everything belongs.

2. **Applicant:** I will use the district guidelines and my grade level scope and sequence charts. I also use the suggested objectives in our adopted textbook series.

3. **Applicant:** I feel that homework is important. It teaches kids to be responsible for planning their time well and for completing jobs on time. I like to grade homework and return it promptly with appropriate feedback.

4. **Applicant:** The research is clear on this topic. Children learn in a variety of ways. I will plan for this by using a variety of methods and strategies that emphasize different modalities (visual, auditory, kinesthetic).

5. **Applicant:** I feel that students need to be made ready for the work force. They need personal attributes of dependability and hard work. They also need basic academic skills of reading at grade level, computing skills and good writing skills for better communication.

pg. 39   The following are sample answers for **Practice Exercise #2**. The responses are *choices of general answers* depending upon *your* preferred orientation.

The Executive Approach
1. **Applicant:** If I were teaching in an elementary intermediate level classroom, my role would be to make sure that every child showed at least one year's growth in his/her skills. I would keep track of everyone's progress so that I could be sure that children who had not mastered a skill could be re-taught that information.

2. **Applicant:** I prefer to use an assertive discipline approach. Each child would know all of the behavior expectations and the consequences for misbehavior. I like to also use a point system for group work so that the group members are kept on task.

3. **Applicant:** My classroom would be well organized. Each child will know where everything goes and how to operate everything. Each child should have a job so that they feel included and learn to have responsibility. I would change the furniture and seating around from time to time to facilitate what the class is doing.

4. **Applicant:** I think that an organized grading system is very important. Students chart their progress on individual progress sheets and wall charts are also used to easily group kids needing help on various skills. Mastery level of at least 80% is expected for all skills. When a child masters an objective he moves on to the next. Kids like this and are motivated by it.

5. **Applicant:** I like to start with the district guidelines for my grade level. Then, I consult with other teachers at my grade and we decide on our grade level scope and sequence. My unit plans reflect this planning but also incorporate the suggestions from the text. My daily plans add the personal touches I like to include that individualize my instruction so all students can achieve.

The Humanist Approach
1. **Applicant:** My job as a teacher for this 2nd grade class is to help the children to grow in whatever ways they need. Each child comes to me with a rich background that is a unique challenge. It is my job to find what the child needs and make sure I can offer him/her a chance to grow.

2. **Applicant:** I believe that each child can be shown how to be a member of our class community. Disagreements and disputes can be negotiated one-to-one. Class meetings are a wonderful forum for airing

problems that affect every single child. More severe individual problems are dealt with on a contract basis where the child and I work out what we can do about improving our mutual environment.

3. **Applicant:** I think it is crucial for kids to love contact with *real* things in their environment. I use authentic literature, so my room is filled with books. Kids *love* to read if given time and space. We have interest centers around the room. I like to have animals that children learn to care for, and plants and collection of objects for kids to examine. I prefer to have my kids at tables rather than individual desks.

4. **Applicant:** I think that we place too much emphasis on grades. I prefer to conference with parents using samples of the kids work. This gives everyone a better idea of what the child can do.

5. **Applicant:** Although I have a very clear idea of the ways I plan to stimulate the kids to think, observe, and examine, I prefer to involve the children in the day to day decisions about what we will study. Children learn best when they are interested and involved in their learning. I don't like to lay down artificial goals for them.

The Classicist Approach
1. **Applicant:** I want to excite kids about English literature. There is such a need for students to do more reading. I have chosen many wonderful books that I know they'll enjoy and be challenged by. Great literature has been a source of both inspiration and comfort to me personally. I'd love to share this with kids.

2. **Applicant:** The first week of class I make it clear what my expectations are and why. Basically kids understand that I'm fair and yet firm. I don't really ever have too many problems. I keep the kids so busy with their reading that they seldom have time to be disruptive.

3. **Applicant:** I think the best thing I can do is to provide *plenty* of good books for them to read. My room is filled with interesting books and I have pictures and biographical information about many of the authors that I display in the classroom.

4. **Applicant:** Grades are important. I let the kids know exactly what they will be responsible for and that if they are thoroughly prepared, they should be able to answer my test questions. I prefer giving essay exams because I think kids stretch more when they have to synthesize information.

5. **Applicant:** I have very extensive lesson plans that bring together ideas from many sources. I do use the text, but I also bring a great deal of supplemental reading.

The Informationist Approach
1. **Applicant:** I think that my role as a teacher will be a role of rapidly increasing importance. Information is being added to our world at exponential rates and kids really need help to figure out how to deal with so much conflicting input. I would like to help them make sense of it all.

2. **Applicant:** Kids will be encouraged to become responsible citizens of this class and school and then of their city, state and beyond. There will be rules that I make and enforce about what the students can and cannot do with all our equipment. There will also be common courtesy rules that we will generate together and enforce as a group.

3. **Applicant:** Luckily this school already has many of the kinds of computer equipment that we will need to really begin to delve into the curriculum. If I am the teacher of this class, I'd try to get *Intel* to donate a rebuilt laser printer that would allow us to create higher-quality material. My goal is to have these kids ready for the world of work.

4. **Applicant:** Grades will be a reflection of the quality of work that each student creates. Although students will be expected to show adequate progress on their standardized tests, I am most concerned about how well they apply their knowledge in their daily work.

5. **Applicant:** Since my plans for every student will be varied in accordance with their performance levels, I will be using many resources to help me in my planning process. Part of what I hope my students will learn is that there are multiple sources from which we can all learn... film, books, on-line, community members and each other.

REFERENCES

Adler, M. (1993). *The four dimensions of philosophy*: Metaphysical, moral, objective, categorical. New York: Macmillan.

Anderson, R., & Ortony, A. (1975) On putting apple into bottles: A problem of polysemy. *Cognition Psychology, 7,* 167-180.

Barron's Educational Series, Inc. (1993). *Better Resumes for Sales & Marketing Personnel.*

Berliner, D. (1983). The Executive Functions of Teaching. *Instructor, 9,* 29-39.

Bogdan, R., & Bicklan, S. (1982). *Qualitative research for education: An introduction to theory and methods.* Boston: Allyn & Bacon.

Bousfield, W.A. (1953). The occurrence of clustering in recall of randomly arranged associates. *Journal of General Psychology, 49,* 229-240.

Bransford, J.D., & Johnson, M.K. (1972). Contextual prerequisites for understanding: Some investigations of comprehension and recall. *Journal of Verbal Learning and Verbal Behavior, 11,* 717-726.

Bransford, J.D., Barclay, J.R., & Franks, J.J. (1972) Sentence memory: A constructive versus interpretative approach. *Cognitive Psychology, 3,* 193-203.

Canter, L. & Canter, M. (1992). *Assertive discipline: Positive behavior management for today's classroom.* 2nd ed. Santa Monica, CA: Lee Canter & Associates.

Chomsky, N. (1959). Review of Skinner's Verbal Behavior. *Language, 35,* 26-58.

Davis, O. (1982). A conversation with Mortimer Adler. *Educational Leadership.* 39 (8). 579-80.

Dewey, J. (1964). *Demoncracy in Education.* New York:Macmilan.

Doll Jr., W. (1993a). *A post-modern perspective on curriculum.* New York: Teachers College Pres.

Doll Jr., W. (1993b). Curriculum possibilities in a "post"-future. *Journal of Curriculum and Supervision* 8(4), 277-292.

Downs, R. (1975). *Heinrich Pestalozzi: Father of modern pedagogy.* New York:Twayne.

Enz, B.J. (1997). *Teachers, how to market yourself effectively.* Des Moines, IA: Kendall-Hunt.

Feinberg, W. & Soltis, J. (1992). *School and society.* New York: Teachers College Press.

Fenstermacher, G., & Soltis, J. (1986). *Approaches to teaching.* New York: Teachers College Press.

Fenstermacher, G., & Soltis, J. (1992). *Approaches to teaching.* New York: Teachers College Press.

Freire, P. (1970). Pedagogy of the oppressed. (M.B. Ramso, Trans.). New York: Seabury Press.

Ginott, H. (1971). *Teacher and child.* New York: Macmillan.

Hutchins, R. (1952). *Great books of the western world.* In *The New Encyclopedia Britannica.* V 20, 24-26. Chicago: Encyclopedia Britannica.

Hunter, M. (1971). *Teach for transfer.* El Segundo: CA. TIP Publications.

Kohn, A. (1997). *How not to teach values: a critical look at character education.* Phi Delta Kappan. 78:6.

Lawerence, E. (1953). *Fredrich Froebel and English Education.* New York: Philosophical Library, Inc.

Maslow, A. (1970). *Motivation and Personality.* 2nd ed. New York: Harper & Row.

Mead, M. (1951). *The School in American Culture.* Cambridge, Mass.: Harvard University Press.

MacDonald, B. (1995). *Theory as a prayerful act.* New York: Peter Lang.

Oliva, P. (1986). *Developing the curriculum.* 2nd ed. New York: Harper Collins.

Ravitch, D. (1984). *The troubled crusade: American education 1945-1980.*

Richelle, M. (1993). *B.F. Skinner: A Reappraisal.* Hove (UK): Lawrence Erlbaum Associates, 171-172.

Rogers, C. (1969). *Freedom to learn.* Columbus, Ohio: Charles E. Merrill.

Rogers, C. (1980). *A way of being.* New York: Houghton Mifflen.

Sachs, J.S. (1967). Recognition memory for syntactic and semantic aspects of connected discourse. *Perception and Psycholphysics, 2,* 437-442.

Schwartz, S.H. & Bilsky, W. (1987). Toward a psychological structure of human values. *Journal of Personality and Social Pyschology, 53,* 550-562.

Skinner, B.F. (1968). *The technology of teaching.* New York: Appleton-Century-Crofts.

Slattery, P. (1995a). *Curriculum development in the postmodern era.* New York: Garland.

Slattery, P. (1995b). *Time and education: Postmodern eschatological perspectives.* Paper presented at the 1995 annual meeting of the american Educational Research Association. San Francisco.

Smith, M. (1984). *Lives in Education.* Iowa State University Press.

Taba, H. (1962). *Curriculum development: Theory and practice.* New York: Harcourt Brace Jovanovich.

Wactler, C. (1990). *How student teachers make sense of teaching: The derivations of an individual's educational philosophy.* Unpublished doctoral dissertation, Arizona State University, Tempe, Arizona.

Westbrook, R. (1991). *John Dewey and American democracy.* Ithaca, New York: Cornell University Press, 6-9.